Lament for a Son

NICHOLAS WOLTERSTORFF

WILLIAM B. EERDMANS PUBLISHING COMPANY
GRAND RAPIDS, MICHIGAN

Copyright © 1987 by Wm. B. Eerdmans Publishing Co.
255 Jefferson Ave. S.E., Grand Rapids, Mich. 49503

Reprinted, August 1987

Library of Congress Cataloging-in-Publication Data:

Wolterstorff, Nicholas.
  Lament for a son.

  1. Children—Death—Psychological aspects.
2. Bereavement—Psychological aspects. 3. Fathers and
sons. 4. Wolterstorff, Nicholas—Family. 5. Fathers—
United States—Biography. I. Title.
BF575.G7W65 1987   155.9'37   87-8990

ISBN 0-8028-0294-x

The passages quoted on pages 87 and 95 are from *A Letter of
Consolation,* © 1982 by Henri J. M. Nouwen. Used by permis-
sion of Harper & Row, Publishers.

for Eric
JANUARY 31, 1958–JUNE 11, 1983

and to his mother, Claire
his sister, Amy
his brothers, Robert, Klaas, and Christopher

"I can't wait to get back to the mountains again."
—ERW in a letter to JR

Preface

I wrote the following to honor our son and brother Eric, who died in a mountain-climbing accident in Austria in his twenty-fifth year, and to voice my grief. Though it is intensely personal, I have decided now to publish it, in the hope that it will be of help to some of those who find themselves with us in the company of mourners.

Born on a snowy night in New Haven, he died twenty-five years later on a snowy slope in the Kaisergebirger. Tenderly we laid him in warm June earth. Willows were releasing their seeds of puffy white, blanketing the ground.

I catch myself: Was it *him* we laid in the earth? I had touched his cheek. Its cold still hardness pushed me back. Death, I knew, was cold. And death was still. But nobody had mentioned that all the softness went out. His spirit had departed and taken along the warmth and activity and, yes, the softness. *He* was gone. "Eric, where are you?" But I am not very good at separating person from body. Maybe that comes with practice. The red hair, the dimples, the chipmunky look—that *was* Eric.

THE CALL CAME at 3:30 on that Sunday after-noon, a bright sunny day. We had just sent a younger brother off to the plane to be with him for the summer.

"Mr. Wolterstorff?"

"Yes."

"Is this Eric's father?"

"Yes."

"Mr. Wolterstorff, I must give you some bad news."

"Yes."

"Eric has been climbing in the mountains and has had an accident."

"Yes."

"Eric has had a serious accident."

"Yes."

"Mr. Wolterstorff, I must tell you, Eric is dead. Mr. Wolterstorff, are you there? You must come at once! Mr. Wolterstorff, Eric is dead."

For three seconds I felt the peace of resig-nation: arms extended, limp son in hand, peace-fully offering him to someone—Someone. Then the pain—cold burning pain.

He was, like all our children, always quick and bright. He entered college as a National Merit Scholar. Excellent at science and math, he spent his college summers in computer programming. Eventually, he decided to go into art history rather than science; there, he felt, he touched humanity. He was a fine artist himself, an accomplished potter, knowledgeable in music, good in performance.

He was a hard worker, not disposed to waste his time—perhaps too much so, too little inclined to savor or even tolerate interruptions, too much oriented toward his goals, not inclined enough to humor. He gave up potting because it didn't fit into his plans. Still, he knew delight. He was venturesome, traveling on his own throughout much of the world, never shrinking from a challenge or turning aside from the exploration of fresh terrain, inclined to overestimate his physical skills and strength. At ten he almost drowned, not willing to admit that he could barely swim. He lived intensely.

On Thanksgiving Day the pastor spoke of acquiring a grateful eye. Eric's was a grateful eye—and ear and mind. Not just a delighting eye but a grateful one. He was a person of faith. Once when little—six years old, perhaps—as he was riding in the car with me somewhere he asked, "Dad, how do we know there's God?" He asked the question, but I don't think he ever seriously doubted. He loved to worship in the company of a genuine community. He died in the Lord.

He put his stamp on things. I think of the poet Gerard Manley Hopkins's notion of inscape: a thing had inscape for Hopkins when it had some definite character. In one of his letters Hopkins speaks of the pain he felt when a tree in the garden, full of inscape, was chopped down. Eric put inscape on things: the way he dressed, the way he cooked, the way he shook hands, the way he answered the phone. "And I wished to die and not to see the inscapes of the world destroyed any more."

When I got angry with him, it was usually over his self-centeredness. Though he spent much of one summer helping rebuild the houses of tornado victims, he was grumpy when I took him along to help build our cabin. I remember being surprised when, without being asked, he cheerfully helped carry our suitcases through the Chicago train station when he was a young teenager.

In his latter years there was in him a loneliness, an inner solitude. What gave him most delight was friends—close friends to whom he could speak of what he most deeply thought and felt and believed. He always longed for those fleeting moments with friends when there is no longer any gap between them. He saw his old friends drifting off to other places and other interests, getting married. His deep longing for intimacy left him lonely.

He was loyal, and principled to a fault— too severe, sometimes too stern and critical, too little accepting of humanity's warts. That gave him trouble in human relationships. Yet he could be gentle and loving. His landlady in Munich told how his face lit up when he learned that his brother was to be with him for the summer. He eagerly anticipated holidays with the family, telling me once how this surprised his friends in graduate school.

And he loved the mountains, loved them passionately. "Über alles," said his landlady. That was not quite true. He loved friends more. But the mountains lured and beckoned him irresistibly. Much as he loved the art and cathedrals of Europe, he loved the mountains more.

His love was his death.

We took him too much for granted. Perhaps we all take each other too much for granted. The routines of life distract us; our own pursuits make us oblivious; our anxieties and sorrows, unmindful. The beauties of the familiar go unremarked. We do not treasure each other enough.

He was a gift to us for twenty-five years. When the gift was finally snatched away, I realized how great it was. Then I could not tell him. An outpouring of letters arrived, many expressing appreciation for Eric. They all made me weep again: each word of praise a stab of loss.

How can I be thankful, in his gone-ness, for what he was? I find I am. But the pain of the *no more* outweighs the gratitude of the *once was*. Will it always be so?

I didn't know how much I loved him until he was gone.

Is love like that?

GONE FROM THE face of the earth. I wait for a group of students to cross the street, and suddenly I think: He is not there. I go to a ballgame and find myself singling out the twenty-five-year olds; none of them is he. In all the crowds and streets and rooms and churches and schools and libraries and gatherings of friends in our world, on all the mountains, I will not find him. Only his absence.

Silence. "Was there a letter from Eric today?" "When did Eric say he would call?" Now only silence. Absence and silence.

When we gather now there's always someone missing, his absence as present as our presence, his silence as loud as our speech. Still five children, but one always gone.

When we're all together, we're not all together.

IT'S THE *neverness* that is so painful. *Never again* to be here with us—never to sit with us at table, never to travel with us, never to laugh with us, never to cry with us, never to embrace us as he leaves for school, never to see his brothers and sister marry. All the rest of our lives we must live without him. Only our death can stop the pain of his death.

A month, a year, five years—with that I could live. But not this forever.

I step outdoors into the moist moldly fragrance of an early summer morning and arm in arm with my enjoyment comes the realization that never again will he smell this.

As a cloud vanishes and is gone,
   so he who goes down to the grave does
      not return,
He will never come to his house again;
   his place will know him no more.

JOB 7:9-10

One small misstep and now this endless neverness.

IT'S SO WRONG, so profoundly wrong, for a child to die before its parents. It's hard enough to bury our parents. But that we expect. Our parents belong to our past, our children belong to our future. We do not visualize our future without them. How can I bury my son, my future, one of the next in line? He was meant to bury me!

I HAD TO FLY across the ocean to claim his body. Grim duty. It *had* been his body. Now it was mine to claim, mine to sign documents of release for, mine to take ownership of. The plane was full of youths going to Europe for their first time—loud, boisterous, exuberant. I burrowed into my seat.

My friend Bernhard met me. Together we went to Eric's apartment in Munich. There we met four of his friends. They had arrived that morning brightly asking the landlady if they could see Eric. "No, I'm afraid you can't. He's dead."

Everything in his room spoke of him— light and airy, prints on the walls, art books and mountaineering books on the table, Indonesian spices in the cupboard, everything neat. *Inscape*. But where is the person who arranged these things? Where is the life that gave them meaning? His clothes hang limp.

We went to Kufstein to reclaim his body. The undertaker advised against seeing it. I saw him bumping, scraping, crashing down the mountain, grasping for a hold, missing, knowing he was to die, mutilated. They handed me his boots and backpack unscathed. Cruel mockery! The one we loved torn, bleeding, wounded, broken, dead. These shoes, this pack—bright and fresh, none the worse. "We're ready for the next climb. What's the holdup?"

Tell it to the people who make them, put it in the ads of those who sell them—"Know that if you bump and scrape to your death on a mountain, these shoes will come through unscathed, ready to be worn again by family and friends."

> Man born of woman
>   is of few days and full of trouble.
> He springs up like a flower and withers
>   away;
>   like a fleeting shadow, he does not
>   endure.

JOB 14:1-2

The flower withers, the "effects" remain.

WHY DID HE do it? Why did he climb that mountain? Why didn't he stay on flat earth? Why did he climb it alone? Why didn't he go with someone, roped up safely?

I know the answers. He climbed alone because in the mountains he preferred solitude to the chatter of those he did not know. Climbing with friends was what he liked most. But if friends were lacking, he preferred solitude. The guidebook gave no hint that it wasn't safe to climb alone.

But why did he climb at all? What was it about the mountains that drew him? I suspect that only those who themselves climb can really know. I can only imagine.

He was lured by the exhilaration of meeting head-on the intellectual and physical challenge of climbing. Perhaps in nothing else are mind and body so joined in being taxed. And he was gripped by the awesome sublimity of the mountains: not some 3″ by 5″ two-dimensional beauty on which we carefully focus our attention, but a beauty all-encompassing, unavoidable. Beauty pure from the hand of God, untouched by human hand. And deepest, perhaps, climbing was for him a spiritual experience. To go into the mountains was to face God.

Challenge, sublimity, purity, spirituality—and mingled with these, menace. To us soft, small, fragile, unsurefooted creatures scrambling over them, the mountains are menacingly indifferent. How insipid it would be if every misstep, every slip of the hand, meant no more than a five-foot drop into an Alpine meadow. The menace is essential to the exhilaration of achievement. On the way up he passed a huge boulder onto which were fixed plaques with names of over fifty people who had died on the trio of mountains one of which he was about to climb. He must have seen it.

So I know why he went. His deepest self drew him there, a self his mother and I helped to shape. He had learned of challenge, of delight, of God. Something of us was inching its way up that mountain on that brilliant Saturday in June. Something of us slid down, bones crushed.

But the question keeps asking itself, "Why did he do it?"

HE WAS WRITING a thesis on the origins of modern architecture. In the 1920s there was a furious dispute, especially in and around the Bauhaus in Germany, over the future direction of architecture. The winners of the dispute at the time were those who promoted the International Style. They favored the use of the latest technologies, and were devoted to the reconstruction of cities in accord with "good planning principles." The losers, who favored local indigenous architecture, were sceptical of this rationalist ideal of reconstructing cities according to the good planning principles of architects. They thought that the use of new technologies and materials should be tempered by respect for tried and tested local materials and techniques.

Eric's project was to explore the ideas and building practices of those losers, especially of the most gifted of them, Paul Schultze-Naumberg. His project was never finished. His notes lie mute in boxes. They never got their voice.

Does that matter? Most human beings do not contribute to the cultural deposit of humanity. They live out lives of routine as farmers, as housewives, as factory workers, as husbands, as mothers, as fathers; after two or three generations the earth knows of them no more. Others make creative additions to culture, things that get passed on through time. Would Eric's project have been such an addition? I do not know. Does it matter? Is his death to be lamented more than the death of another twenty-five-year old who spent his life in routine but through that routine loved those he knew, trusted God, and cherished the earth? What is it that we carry into God's abiding kingdom? Is it only love and faith and trust? Or is it culture too?

I lament all that might have been, and now will never be.

I STAND BEFORE the library, where he spent so many days of his last months. He's walking up these steps, through those doors, to the desk, asking for a book, receiving it, sitting down at a table—which one?—copying out these notes I have.

No, I see nothing; no form at all, not even a trace. All bone and muscle gone, the steps swept clear—no smile, no sturdy step, no bright intelligence, no silhouette, no love embodied. Where he should be, I stare straight through.

Turn it back. Stop the clock and turn it back, back to that last Friday, that last Saturday. Let him do it over: get up late this time, too late to climb, read a book, wait for his brother. Let him do it right this time. Let us all do it right.

It won't stop; it keeps on going, unforgiving, unrelenting. The gears and brakes are gone. There's nothing I can do to make it stop. Farther back and farther yet, back into the dimming past. The gap begins to gape.

Is there no one who can slow it down, make it stop, turn it back? Must we all be swept forever on, away, beyond, beauty lost, and love, sorrow hard on sorrow, until the measure of our losses has been filled?

HE WAS cut down at the peak of vitality and promise. He had finished his research and was ready to write. We found the outline on top of his notes. Friends who had visited him a week earlier said they had never seen him so enthusiastic. He was looking forward to climbing the Matterhorn with friends late in the summer and was getting himself into condition, running and doing practice climbs.

Is the death of a child any easier when vitality has wound down? If some disease had wasted him away, sapped his energy, made him weak, would death then have seemed a proper closure? But then all the pain would have been in seeing the winding down. Is it easier when good-byes have been said? We never said good-bye to Eric.

Each death is as unique as each life. Each has its own stamp. Inscape. The tree in Hopkins's garden had an inscape, but so did the felling of the tree. And one child's death differs from another not in the intensity of the pain it causes but in the quality. To see a young life wither and die is as painful as to see it snapped off.

The son of a friend—same age as Eric—died a few weeks before Eric. The friend's son committed suicide. The pain of his life was so intense that he took the life that gave the pain. I thought for a time that such a death must be easier to bear than the death of one with zest for life. He wanted to die. When I talked to the father, I saw that I was wrong.

Death is the great leveller, so our writers have always told us. Of course they are right. But they have neglected to mention the uniqueness of each death—and the solitude of suffering which accompanies that uniqueness. We say, "I know how you are feeling." But we don't.

ON THE WAY back I thought about tears. Our culture says that men must be strong and that the strength of a man in sorrow is to be seen in his tearless face. Tears are for women. Tears are signs of weakness and women are permitted to be weak. Of course it's better if they too are strong.

But why celebrate stoic tearlessness? Why insist on never outwarding the inward when that inward is bleeding? Does enduring while crying not require as much strength as never crying? Must we always mask our suffering? May we not sometimes allow people to see and enter it? I mean, may *men* not do this?

And why is it so important to act strong? I have been graced with the strength to endure. But I have been assaulted, and in the assault wounded, grievously wounded. Am I to pretend otherwise? Wounds are ugly, I know. They repel. But must they always be swathed?

I shall look at the world through tears. Perhaps I shall see things that dry-eyed I could not see.

"THE TEARS . . . streamed down, and I let them flow as freely as they would, making of them a pillow for my heart. On them it rested."

—AUGUSTINE,
Confessions IX, 12

IT WAS LATE at night when I returned home, but I assembled the family. I remember only what I said first and last. "Our Eric is gone," I said. And at the end, that we now must learn to live as faithfully and authentically with Eric gone as we had tried to do with Eric present.

How do we do that? And what does it mean? It will take a long time to learn.

It means not forgetting him. It means speaking of him. It means remembering him. *Remembering:* one of the profoundest features of the Christian and Jewish way of being-in-the-world and being-in-history is remembering. "Remember," "do not forget," "do this as a remembrance." We are to hold the past in remembrance and not let it slide away. For in history we find God.

If Eric's life was a gift, surely then we are to hold it in remembrance—to resist amnesia, to renounce oblivion.

All around us are his things: his clothes, his books, his camera, the things he made—pots, drawings, slides, photos, notes, papers. They speak with forked tongue, words of joyful pride and words of sorrow. Do we put them all behind doors to muffle the sorrow or leave them out to hear them tell of the hands that shaped them?

We shall leave them out. We will not store the pots, not turn the photos. We will put them where they confront us. This as a remembrance, as a memorial.

WE FOUND LISTS of things he was planning to do: plans, intentions, proposed undertakings, breathing hope. Now they're all spilled out, shattered on those rough rocks. To be human is to remember, to carry the past along into the present. Even more, to be human is to look ahead, to expect, to envision. To be human is to expect while remembering, to plan while recollecting. A baby looks neither back nor ahead; her humanity is just beginning. An old person scarcely looks ahead; his plans are cautious, few, short-term. And when memory also fails, then humanity is diminished to the point of disappearance. Eric was bursting with futurity—with plans and resolutions. Humanity in full flower. Now it's all gone. All the rich future that he held—gone in those tumbling seconds. His death is things to do not done—never to be done.

ELEMENTS OF THE gospel which I had always thought would console did not. They did something else, something important, but not that. It did not console me to be reminded of the hope of resurrection. If I had forgotten that hope, then it would indeed have brought light into my life to be reminded of it. But I did not think of death as a bottomless pit. I did not grieve as one who has no hope. Yet Eric is gone, *here* and *now* he is gone; *now* I cannot talk with him, *now* I cannot see him, *now* I cannot hug him, *now* I cannot hear of his plans for the future. *That* is my sorrow. A friend said, "Remember, he's in good hands." I was deeply moved. But that reality does not put Eric back in my hands now. That's my grief. For that grief, what consolation can there be other than having him back?

In our day we have come to see again some dimensions of the Bible overlooked for centuries. We have come to see its affirmation of the goodness of creation. God made us embodied historical creatures and affirmed the goodness of that. We are not to yearn for timeless disembodiment.

But this makes death all the more difficult to live with. When death is no longer seen as release from this miserable materiality into our rightful immateriality, when death is seen rather as the slicing off of what God declared to be, and what all of us feel to be, of great worth, then death is—well, not friend but enemy. Though I shall indeed recall that death is being overcome, my grief is that death still stalks this world and one day knifed down my Eric.

Nothing fills the void of his absence. He's not replaceable. We can't go out and get another just like him.

THERE'S A HOLE in the world now. In the place where he was, there's now just nothing. A center, like no other, of memory and hope and knowledge and affection which once inhabited this earth is gone. Only a gap remains. A perspective on this world unique in this world which once moved about within this world has been rubbed out. Only a void is left. There's nobody now who saw just what he saw, knows what he knew, remembers what he remembered, loves what he loved. A person, an irreplaceable person, is gone. Never again will anyone apprehend the world quite the way he did. Never again will anyone inhabit the world the way he did. Questions I have can never now get answers. The world is emptier. My son is gone. Only a hole remains, a void, a gap, never to be filled.

WHAT DO YOU say to someone who is suffering? Some people are gifted with words of wisdom. For such, one is profoundly grateful. There were many such for us. But not all are gifted in that way. Some blurted out strange, inept things. That's OK too. Your words don't have to be wise. The heart that speaks is heard more than the words spoken. And if you can't think of anything at all to say, just say, "I can't think of anything to say. But I want you to know that we are with you in your grief."

Or even, just embrace. Not even the best of words can take away the pain. What words can do is testify that there is more than pain in our journey on earth to a new day. Of those things that are more, the greatest is love. Express your love. How appallingly grim must be the death of a child in the absence of love.

But please: Don't say it's not really so bad. Because it is. Death is awful, demonic. If you think your task as comforter is to tell me that really, all things considered, it's not so bad, you do not sit with me in my grief but place yourself off in the distance away from me. Over there, you are of no help. What I need to hear from you is that you recognize how painful it is. I need to hear from you that you are with me in my desperation. To comfort me, you have to come close. Come sit beside me on my mourning bench.

I know: People do sometimes think things are more awful than they really are. Such people need to be corrected—gently, eventually. But no one thinks death is more awful than it is. It's those who think it's not so bad that need correcting.

Some say nothing because they find the topic too painful for themselves. They fear they will break down. So they put on a brave face and lid their feelings—never reflecting, I suppose, that this adds new pain to the sorrow of their suffering friends. Your tears are salve on our wound, your silence is salt.

And later, when you ask me how I am doing and I respond with a quick, thoughtless "Fine" or "OK," stop me sometime and ask, "No, I mean *really*."

WITH THESE HANDS I lifted him from his cradle—tiny then, soft, warm, and squirming with life. Now at the end with these same hands I touched him in his coffin.

I hesitated: could I bear the pain of this final gesture? In Kufstein I never saw his body. It was too badly mangled, the officers said. But when his body arrived back on Saturday, Claire insisted on seeing it. She was right. I pity those who never get a chance to see and feel the deadness of the one they love, who must *think* death but cannot *sense* it. To fully persuade us of death's reality, and of its grim finality, our eyes and hands must rub against death's cold, hard body, body against body, painfully. Knowing death with mind alone is less than fully knowing it.

Seeing and touching was also a way of taking leave. Not a full leave-taking—not one in which two *persons* said good-bye to each other. But still, a leave-taking. For though we aren't our bodies, yet of nothing on earth do we have more intimate possession than these. Only through these do we dwell here. I knew Eric through his body. In touching the place of his dwelling, I took leave of him—just as in touching him in his crib, I welcomed him to life. Greeting and leave-taking go best, I think, when we do them with our hands.

What showed in the coffin was his face,

and that was not mangled—just some scratches here and there and blood in his hair. Amy said he looked as if he knew something we didn't know. That reminded me that from youth already he had a tendency to act as if he "knew it all."

I DREADED the prospect, but the funeral gave rest to my soul. It did not console me for Eric's absence. Instead it sank deep into me the realization that my son's death is not all there is.

I had myself, a few years earlier, composed the liturgy we used, adapting it from the funeral liturgy of the Catholic church. A friend of ours was suffering from brain cancer; her husband asked me to compose a liturgy for her funeral. At the time I had the vague intimation that her funeral would not be the first occasion for its use. Never did it occur to me that I had composed it for my own son. She who suffers from cancer was present at Eric's funeral.

It was a liturgy which both thanked God for the presence of Eric among us and expressed our grief upon his no longer being present. It sang of the hope of resurrection. It opened with these words:

> When we were baptized in the name of Jesus Christ, we were baptized into his death and buried with him, so that as Christ was raised from the dead by the glory of the Father, we too might live a new life. For if we have been united with him in a death like his, we shall certainly also be united with him in a resurrection like his. Those who believe in him, though they die, yet shall they live.

And it closed with these words:

> Into your tender hands, O merciful Savior, we commend your beloved servant, Eric. Acknowledge, we pray you, a sheep of your own fold, a lamb of your own flock, a sinner of your own redeeming. Receive him into the arms of your abiding mercy, into the rest of your everlasting peace, into the glorious company of those who dwell in your light. And may your kingdom of peace come quickly.

It was a liturgy in which not only words, but also actions and symbols, spoke. After the opening words, a shroud was placed over the coffin, simple but wonderfully beautiful, made a few years before by members of our congregation for the funeral of the friend with cancer. This was its first use. On the shroud over the coffin one of Eric's brothers placed lilies. The music was glorious, some of it sung by the congregation, some by the congregation in conjunction with a choir. Much of it was music from the ecumenical community of Taizé (France). The instruments were those that Eric so much loved, cello and recorder.

We celebrated the Eucharist, that sacrament of God's participation in our brokenness. We came forward successively in groups, standing in circles around the coffin, passing the signs of Christ's brokenness to each other. At the end, before we had committed Eric into the tender resurrected resurrecting hands of Jesus, I could not restrain myself from coming forward to express our deep appreciation for this outpouring of love and faith. In the service Claire had read one of the readings—the Song of Hannah. I had turned aside all suggestions that I too participate, convinced that I would not be able to speak. Now here I was, standing in front of that congregation, they too standing, tears streaming down my face and down theirs, tears answering to tears. I asked them to be patient as I tried to speak. I thanked them for their love. And I spoke briefly of Eric. I do not remember what I said—only that he was a bright flower cut down before he bloomed, that I did not know how much I loved him until he died, and that his great love was his death. Afterwards I found I had the voice to sing the final hymn, "For All the Saints." Then we left, I carrying the resurrection candle, Claire beside me, followed by the family and the coffin.

The candle was still burning firmly and brightly as the people began pressing round. The undertakers stirred to take the coffin away. What am I to do now, blow out this symbol of the resurrection of my son? Why had no one foreseen the impossible pain of this the final act?

"But it's only a candle."

"No, it's more than a candle."

I BURIED myself that warm June day. It was me those gardeners lowered on squeaking straps into that hot dry hole, curious neighborhood children looking down in at me, everyone stilled, wind rustling the oaks. It was me over whom we slid that heavy slab, more than I can lift. It was me on whom we shoveled dirt. It was me we left behind, after reading psalms.

WHAT DOES IT mean, Eric dead, removed from our presence, covered with earth, inert? Or is such shattering of love *beyond* meaning for us, the breaking of meaning—mystery, terrible mystery?

"ALL MANKIND is of one author, and is one volume; when one man dies, one chapter is not torn out of the book, but translated into a better language; and every chapter must be so translated; God employs several translators: some pieces are translated by age, some by sickness, some by war, some by justice; but God's hand is in every translation; and his hand shall bind up all our scattered leaves again, for that library where every book shall lie open to one another: As therefore the bell that rings to a sermon calls not upon the preacher only, but upon the congregation to come, so this bell calls us all. . . .

"No man is an island, entire of itself; every man is a piece of the continent, a part of the main; if a clod be washed away by the sea, Europe is the less, as well as if a promontory were, as well as if a manor of thy friends or of thine own were; any man's death diminishes me, because I am involved in mankind; and therefore never send to know for whom the bell tolls; it tolls for thee."

—JOHN DONNE

A MIST WHICH soft breeze drives off,
    a flutter of finch through bushes,
    a fall of snow,
    candle's flickering flame,
    lily of a day's endurance,
so fleeting is our existence.
A slip of the foot,
    swerve,
    gasp,
    growth inside
and we are gone.

"I HEARD A VOICE say 'Cry!' I said, 'What shall I cry?' 'Cry this,' said the voice:

'All flesh is grass,
    and all its beauty is like the flower of the
      field.
The grass withers, the flower fades,
    when the breath of the Lord blows upon it;
    surely the people is grass.'"

—ISAIAH 40

THE WORLD LOOKS different now. The pinks have become purple, the yellows brown. Mountains now wear crosses on their slopes. Hymns and psalms have reordered themselves so that lines I scarcely noticed now leap out: "He will not suffer they foot to stumble." Photographs that once evoked the laughter of delighted reminiscence now cause only pain. Why are the photographs of him as a little boy so incredibly hard for me to look at? This one here, holding a fish longer than he is tall, six years old? Why is it easier to look at him as a grownup? The pleasure of seeing former students is colored by the realization that they were his friends and that while they thrive he rots.

Something is *over*. In the deepest levels of my existence something is finished, done. My life is divided into before and after. A friend of ours whose husband died young said it meant for her that her youth was over. My youth was already over. But I know what she meant. Something is over.

Especially in places where he and I were together this sense of something *being over* washes over me. It happens not so much at home, but other places. A moment in our lives together of special warmth and intimacy and vividness, a moment when I specially prized him, a moment of hope and expectancy and openness to the future: I remember the moment. But instead of lines of memory leading up to his life in the present, they all enter a place of cold inky blackness and never come out. The book slams shut. The story stops, it doesn't finish. The future closes, the hopes get crushed. And now instead of those shiny moments being things we can share together in delighted memory, I, the survivor, have to bear them alone.

So it is with all memories of him. They all lead into that blackness. It's all over, over, over. All I can do is *remember* him. I can't *experience* him. The person to whom these memories are attached is no longer here with me, standing up. He's only in my memory now, not in my life. Nothing new can happen between us. Everything is sealed tight, shut in the past. I'm still here. I have to go on. I have to start over. But this new start is so different from the first. Then I wasn't carrying this load, this thing that's over.

Sometimes I think that happiness is over for me. I look at photos of the past and immediately comes the thought: that's when we were still happy. But I can still laugh, so I guess that isn't quite it. Perhaps what's over is happiness as the fundamental tone of my existence. Now sorrow is that.

Sorrow is no longer the islands but the sea.

"CAN SADNESS be relieved, or can one only pass it by, very slowly? A day in the radiant sunlight and the sky's blue, in the shadow of a proud dark sail, over rustling waves, along new coast-lines, wouldn't that help to get past sadness?— for a while, for that one day at least."

—MARIA DERMOUT,
The Ten Thousand Things

OUT OF MY SELF I traveled on a journey of love and attached this self of mine to Eric, my son. Now he's gone, lost, ripped loose from love; and the ache of loss sinks down, and down, deep down into my soul, deep beyond all telling. How deep do souls go?

Loss is his as well. How very strange! Yet I feel it acutely. His sudden early death is not just our loss but his: the loss of seeing trees, of hearing music, of reading books, of writing books, of walking through cathedrals, of visiting friends, of being with family, of marrying, of going to church, and—dare I say it—of climbing mountains.

STRANGE DREAM: several times over I was walking down the street with friends and suddenly one of them would disappear. Just disappear. I would turn to say something to him and he would be gone.

Eventually the cause of these disappearances became known—an evil, sinister person. Confrontation was necessary. But I quaked in my boots.

Then a reassuring voice: "Have no fear. Do what you must. I'll be with you."

Did something demonic take place there near the peak of the Ellmauerhalt? Or is this a specimen of mythical thinking that "modern man" ought to eliminate from his mind?

In death one faces not love but malevolence.

LET ME TRY again. All these things I recognize. I remember delighting in them—trees, art, house, music, pink morning sky, work well done, flowers, books. I still delight in them. I'm still grateful. But the zest is gone. The passion is cooled, the striving quieted, the longing stilled. My attachment is loosened. No longer do I set my heart on them. I can do without them. They don't matter. Instead of rowing, I float. The joy that comes my way I savor. But the seeking, the clutching, the aiming, is gone. I don't suppose anyone on the outside notices. I go through my paces. What the world gives, I still accept. But what it promises, I no longer reach for.

I've become an alien in the world, shyly touching it as if it's not mine. I don't belong any more. When someone loved leaves home, home becomes mere house.

I WALKED INTO a store. The ordinariness of what I saw repelled me: people putting onions into baskets, squeezing melons, hoisting gallons of milk, clerks ringing up sales. "How are you today?" "Have a good day now." How could everybody be going about their ordinary business when these were no longer ordinary times? I went to my office and along the way saw the secretaries all at their desks and the students all in their seats and the teachers all at their podiums. Do you not know that he slipped and fell and that we sealed him in a box and covered it with dirt and that he can't get out?

I tried to jog and could not. It was too life-affirming. I rode along with friends to go swimming and found myself paralyzed. I tried music. But why is this music all so affirmative? Has it always been like that? Perhaps then a requiem, that glorious *German Requiem* of Brahms. I have to turn it off. There's too little brokenness in it. Is there no music that speaks of our terrible brokenness? That's not what I mean. I mean: Is there no music that *fits* our brokenness? The music that speaks *about* our brokenness is not itself broken. Is there no broken music?

There are those who plunge immediately back into work. I honor them. But I could not do it. And even if I could, I would not. Plunging back at once into the ordinary and the life-affirming could not be my way of honoring my son. It could not be my way of remembering him. It could not be my way of living with faith and authenticity in his absence.

I SKIMMED SOME books on grief. They offered ways of not looking death and pain in the face, ways of turning away from death out there to one's own inner "grief process" and then, on that, laying the heavy hand of rationality. I will not have it so. I will not look away. I will indeed remind myself that there's more to life than pain. I will accept joy. But I will not look away from Eric dead. Its demonic awfulness I will not ignore. I owe that—to him and to God.

IMAGINATION AND THOUGHT are out of phase. Sometimes it's as if he's not dead, just away. I see him. Then thought intervenes and says, "Remember, he's dead now." For twenty-five years I have been imagining what he's doing. That keeps on going. In me now there is this strange flux of spontaneously picturing him and then painfully reminding myself.

And not just picturing; also hearing. For weeks his boxes of books and clothes stood in the entry. I could not bear to move them. Finally, I began carrying them off to the garage. While carrying the fifth box or so I heard his cheerful voice, loud and clear, calling from the entry, "Hey Dad, I'm back."

His hair will always be red in my pictures of him. Only the living age.

I HAVE BEEN daily grateful for the friend who remarked that grief isolates. He did not mean only that I, grieving, am isolated from you, happy. He meant also that *shared* grief isolates the sharers from each other. Though united in that we are grieving, we grieve differently. As each death has its own character, so too each grief over a death has its own character—its own inscape. The dynamics of each person's sorrow must be allowed to work themselves out without judgment. I may find it strange that you should be tearful today but dry-eyed yesterday when my tears were yesterday. But my sorrow is not your sorrow.

There's something more: I must struggle so hard to regain life that I cannot reach out to you. Nor you to me. The one not grieving must touch us both. It's when people are happy that they say, "Let's get together."

WHAT IS IT that makes the death of a child so indescribably painful? I buried my father and that was hard. But nothing at all like this. One expects to bury one's parents; one doesn't expect—not in our day and age—to bury one's children. The burial of one's child is a wrenching alteration of expectations.

But it's more than that. I feel the more but cannot speak it. A child comes into the world weak and vulnerable. From the first minutes of its life, we protect it. It comes into the world without means of sustenance. Immediately we the parents give it of our own. It begins to display feelings and thoughts and choices of its own. We celebrate those and out of our own way of being-in-the-world try to shape and direct and guide them. We give of ourselves to the formation of this other, from helplessness to independence, trying our best to match our mode of giving to the maturing of the child— our giving maturing with the child's maturing. We take it on ourselves to stay with this helpless infant all the way so that it has a future, a future in which we can delight in its delight and sorrow in its sorrow. Our plans and hopes and fears are plans and hopes and fears for it. Along the way we experience the delights and disappointments of watching that future take shape, from babblings to oratory, from flounderings to climbing, from dependence to equality.

And now he's gone. That future which I embraced to myself has been destroyed. He slipped out of my arms. For twenty-five years I guarded and sustained and encouraged him with these hands of mine, helping him to grow and become a man of his own. Then he slipped out and was smashed.

WAS HE special? Did I love him more—more than his sister and brothers? When they see my tears, do they think I loved him more?

I visualize the appallingly cruel choice with which Hitler's henchmen faced Jewish parents: select one of your children for salvation or let all perish. What would I have done? If a parent loved one of her children more, she would pick that one—or would she avoid picking that one, out of blended love and guilt?

I think I would have been immobilized. I love them equally though differently. None is special; or rather, each is special. Each has an inscape in which I delight. I celebrate them all and love them each.

Death has picked him out, not love. Death has made him special. He is special in my grieving. When I give thanks, I mention all five; when I lament, I mention only him. Wounded love is special love, special in its wound. Now I think of him every day; before, I did not. Of the five, only he has a grave.

AN IMAGE haunts me: proceeding across a battlefield, my father now dead, I am up front to draw the fire. I look back, and one of those I was to protect has fallen.

THE WORST DAYS now are holidays: Thanksgiving, Christmas, Easter, Pentecost, birthdays, weddings, January 31—days meant as festivals of happiness and joy now are days of tears. The gap is too great between day and heart. Days of routine I can manage; no songs are expected. But how am I to sing in this desolate land, when there's always one too few?

INNOCENT QUESTIONS make me wince.

"Will the family all be home for Christmas?" What am I to say? "Yes," I say, "we'll all be home."

"What are your children doing now?" I go down the list: Amy, Robert, Klaas, Christopher. But I omit one. Do I call attention to the omission or do I let it pass?

"How many children do you have?" What do I say, "four" or "five"? "Five" I usually say. Sometimes I explain, sometimes I do not.

SOMEONE SAID TO Claire, "I hope you're learning to live at peace with Eric's death." Peace, shalom, salaam. Shalom is the fulness of life in all dimensions. Shalom is dwelling in justice and delight with God, with neighbor, with oneself, in nature. Death is shalom's mortal enemy. Death is demonic. We cannot live at peace with death.

When the writer of *Revelation* spoke of the coming of the day of shalom, he did not say that on that day we would live at peace with death. He said that on that day "There will be no more death or mourning or crying or pain, for the old order of things has passed away."

I shall try to keep the wound from healing, in recognition of our living still in the old order of things. I shall try to keep it from healing, in solidarity with those who sit beside me on humanity's mourning bench.

WHAT DO I DO now with my regrets—over the time I neglected to take him along hiking, over the times I placed work ahead of being with him, over the times I postponed writing letters, over the times I unreasonably got angry with him—over all the times I hurt him, times I noticed the hurt and times I didn't but should have. Over the times he was sad and I saw, but did little or nothing to console. Over all the times I did not prize the inscape of that image of God in our midst which was he; and over all the other times I did but did not tell him so. Over all the times he was something wonderful or did something fine and I was oblivious or silent— sometimes because my own projects were my single-minded pursuit, sometimes because my own worries were my single-minded concern. And sometimes because I did not want his excellence to "go to his head."

What do I do with this basket of regrets? What do I do with my regret that I did not warn him more often and more firmly of the dangers of climbing? When the person is living we can make amends—can say we are sorry, if our pride is not too large to swallow; can change our ways, if our projects are not loved more than the other person. But when the person is dead, what do we do with our regrets?

A friend warned me against this question. Don't rehearse your regrets, he said. But they come to mind unrehearsed. Should I try to stop them? Should I undertake some discipline of memory to stop this parade of all I wish had been different?

No, I will not do that. Putting out of mind is not my way.

I believe that God forgives me. I do not doubt that. The matter between God and me is closed. But what about the matter betwen Eric and me? For my regrets remain. What do I do with my God-forgiven regrets? Maybe some of what I regret doesn't even need forgiving; maybe sometimes I did as well as I could. Full love isn't always possible in this fallen world of ours. Still, I regret.

I shall live with them. I shall accept my regrets as part of my life, to be numbered among my self-inflicted wounds. But I will not endlessly gaze at them. I shall allow the memories to prod me into doing better with those still living. And I shall allow them to sharpen the vision and intensify the hope for that Great Day coming when we can all throw ourselves into each other's arms and say, "I'm sorry."

The God of love will surely grant us such a day. Love needs that.

A FRIEND remarked after the funeral that what he had seen there was the endurance of faith. He added that this is the message of the book of Job. I think he was right about both.

The only thing that angered me in what people offered was a small book someone gave me written by a father whose son had also been killed in a mountaineering accident. The writer said that in his church on the Sunday before his son's death, they had read Psalm 18. He now interpreted verse 36 as speaking to him:

> Thou didst give a wide place for my steps
>   under me,
> and my foot did not slip.

His son's foot had not slipped. *God* had shaken the mountain. God had decided that it was time for him to come home.

I find this pious attitude deaf to the message of the Christian gospel. Death is here understood as a normal instrument of God's dealing with us. "You there have lived out the years I've planned for you, so I'll just shake the mountain a bit. All of you there, I'll send some starlings into the engine of your plane. And as for you there, a stroke while running will do nicely."

The Bible speaks instead of God's *overcoming* death. Paul calls it the last great enemy to be overcome. God is appalled by death. My pain over my son's death is shared by *his* pain over my son's death. And, yes, I share in his pain over *his* son's death.

Seeing God as the agent of death is one way of fitting together into a rational pattern God, ourselves, and death. There are other ways. One of these has been explored in a book by Rabbi Kushner: God too is pained by death, more even than you and I are; but there's nothing much he can do about it.

I cannot fit it all together by saying, "He did it," but neither can I do so by saying, "There was nothing he could do about it." I cannot fit it together at all. I can only, with Job, endure. I do not know why God did not prevent Eric's death. To live without the answer is precarious. It's hard to keep one's footing.

Job's friends tried out on him their answer. "God did it, Job; he was the agent of your children's death. He did it because of some wickedness in you; he did it to punish you. Nothing indeed in your public life would seem to merit such retribution; it must then be something in your private inner life. Tell us what it is, Job. Confess."

The writer of Job refuses to say that God views the lives and deaths of children as cats-o'-nine-tails with which to lacerate parents.

I have no explanation. I can do nothing else than endure in the face of this deepest and most painful of mysteries. I believe in God the Father Almighty, maker of heaven and earth and resurrecter of Jesus Christ. I also believe that my son's life was cut off in its prime. I cannot fit these pieces together. I am at a loss. I have read the theodicies produced to justify the ways of God to man. I find them unconvincing. To the most agonized question I have ever asked I do not know the answer. I do not know why God would watch him fall. I do not know why God would watch me wounded. I cannot even guess.

C. S. Lewis, writing about the death of his wife, was plainly angry with God. He, Lewis, deserved something better than to be treated so shabbily. I am not angry but baffled and hurt. My wound is an unanswered question. The wounds of all humanity are an unanswered question.

I AM AT AN impasse, and you, O God, have brought me here. From my earliest days, I heard of you. From my earliest days, I believed in you. I shared in the life of your people: in their prayers, in their work, in their songs, in their listening for your speech and in their watching for your presence. For me your yoke was easy. On me your presence smiled.

Noon has darkened. As fast as she could say, "He's dead," the light dimmed. And where are you in this darkness? I learned to spy you in the light. Here in this darkness I cannot find you. If I had never looked for you, or looked but never found, I would not feel this pain of your absence. Or is it not your absence in which I dwell but your elusive troubling presence?

Will my eyes adjust to this darkness? Will I find you in the dark—not in the streaks of light which remain, but in the darkness? Has anyone ever found you there? Did they love what they saw? Did they see love? And are there songs for singing when the light has gone dim? The songs I learned were all of praise and thanksgiving and repentance. Or in the dark, is it best to wait in silence?

FAITH ENDURES; but my address to God is uncomfortably, perplexingly, altered. It's off-target, qualified. I want to ask for Eric back. But I can't. So I aim around the bull's-eye. I want to ask that God protect the members of my family. But I asked that for Eric.

I must explore The Lament as a mode for my address to God. Psalm 42 is a lament in the context of a faith that endures. Lament and trust are in tension, like wood and string in bow.

> My tears have been my food day and
> night,

says the songwriter. I remember, he says, how it was when joy was still my lot,

> how I used to go with the multitude,
> leading the procession to the house of
> God,
> with shouts of joy and thanksgiving
> among the festive throng.

Now it's different. I am downcast, disturbed. Yet I find that faith is not dead. So I say to myself,

> Put your hope in God,
> for I will yet praise him,
> my Savior and my God.

But then my grief returns and again I lament, to God my Rock:

70

Why have you forgotten me?
Why must I go about mourning,
    oppressed by the enemy?

Again faith replies:

    Put your hope in God,
        for I will yet praise him,
        my Savior and my God.

Back and forth, lament and faith, faith and lament, each fastened to the other. A bruised
faith, a longing faith, a faith emptied of near-
ness:

    As the deer pants for streams of water,
        so my soul pants for you, O God.
    My soul thirsts for God, for the living
        God.
    When can I go and meet with God?

Yet in the distance of endurance I join the song:

    By day the Lord directs his love,
        at night his song is with me—
        a prayer to the God of my life.

Have you changed, someone asked. He did not mean whether the world looks different to me now. He meant whether my character has changed. Have *I* changed?

The suffering of the world has worked its way deeper inside me. I never knew that sorrow could be like this. Six months before, I had gone to the funeral of the twenty-three-year-old son of friends. I tried to imagine the quality of their grief. I know now that I failed miserably.

Each person's suffering has its own quality. No outsider can ever fully enter it. Yet more of suffering is now accessible to me. I still don't fully know what it's like to be one of those mothers one sees in poverty posters, soup tin in hand, bloated child alongside, utterly dependent for her very existence on the largesse of others. I still don't fully know what it's like to be a member of a people whose whole national existence is under attack, Armenian or Jew or Palestinian. Yet I now know more of it.

And I know now about helplessness—of what to do when there is nothing to do. I have learned coping. We live in a time and place where, over and over, when confronted with something unpleasant we pursue not coping but overcoming. Often we succeed. Most of humanity has not enjoyed and does not enjoy such luxury. Death shatters our illusion that we can make do without coping. When we have overcome absence with phone calls, winglessness with airplanes, summer heat with air-conditioning—when we have overcome all these and much more besides, then there will abide two things with which we must cope: the evil in our hearts and death. There are those who vainly think that some technology will even enable us to overcome the former. Everyone knows that there is no technology for overcoming death. Death is left for God's overcoming.

I have changed, yes. For the better, I do not doubt. But without a moment's hesitation I would exchange those changes for Eric back.

I HAVE COME to see that the Christian gospel tells us more of the meaning of sin than of suffering. Of sin it says that its root lies not in God but in the will of the human being. It is true that an inclination toward lovelessness and injustice is now mysteriously perpetuated down through the generations. But it remains an inclination, not a necessity. Sin belongs to us. To this the gospel adds that our lovelessness pains God; it grieves him. And then the good news: God's response to this pain is forgiveness—not avenging fury but forgiveness. Jesus Christ is the announcement: the Master of the Universe forgives.

To the "why" of suffering we get no firm answer. Of course some suffering is easily seen to be the result of our sin: war, assault, poverty amidst plenty, the hurtful word. And maybe some is chastisement. But not all. The meaning of the remainder is not told us. It eludes us. Our net of meaning is too small. There's more to our suffering than our guilt.

"TRULY, YOU ARE a God who hides yourself, O God of Israel, the Savior" (Isa. 45:15).

"A religion which does not affirm that God is hidden is not true. *Vere tu es Deus absconditus*—truly you are a hidden God" (Pascal).

Perhaps it has been a mistake to think that God reveals himself. He speaks, yes. But as he speaks, he hides. His face he does not show us.

WHY DON'T YOU just scrap this God business, says one of my bitter suffering friends. It's a rotten world, you and I have been shafted, and that's that.

I'm pinned down. When I survey this gigantic intricate world, I cannot believe that it just came about. I do not mean that I have some good arguments for its being made and that I believe in the arguments. I mean that this conviction wells up irresistibly within me when I contemplate the world. The experiment of trying to abolish it does not work. When looking at the heavens, I cannot manage to believe that they do not declare the glory of God. When looking at the earth, I cannot bring off the attempt to believe that it does not display his handiwork.

And when I read the New Testament and look into the material surrounding it, I am convinced that the man Jesus of Nazareth was raised from the dead. In that, I see the sign that he was more than a prophet. He was the Son of God.

Faith is a footbridge that you don't know will hold you up over the chasm until you're forced to walk out onto it. I'm standing there now, over the chasm. I inspect the bridge. Am I deluded in believing that in God the question shouted out by the wounds of the world has its answer? Am I deluded in believing that someday I will know the answer? Am I deluded in believing that once I know the answer, I will see that love has conquered?

I cannot dispel the sense of conducting my inspection in the presence of the Creating/ Resurrecting One.

WITH EVERY FIBER of my being I long to talk with Eric again. When I mentioned this to someone, she asked what I would say. I don't know. Maybe I would just blurt out something silly. That would be good enough for a beginning. We could take it from there. Every day I wonder, and some days I doubt, whether that talk will ever take place. But then comes that insistent voice: "Remember, I made all this and raised my own son from the dead, so I can also. . . ."

"I know, I know. But why don't you raise mine now? Why did you ever let him die? If creation took just six days, why does re-creation take so agonizingly long? If your conquest of primeval chaos went so quickly, why must your conquest of sin and death and suffering be so achingly slow?"

When I say my first words to Eric, then God's reign will be here.

WE ARE surrounded by death. As we walk through the grasslands of life it lurks everywhere—behind, to the left, to the right, ahead, everywhere in the swaying grass. Before, I saw it only here and there. The light was too bright. Here in this dim light the dead show up: teachers, colleagues, the children of friends, aunts, uncles, mother, father, the composers whose music I hear, the psalmists whose words I quote, the philosophers whose texts I read, the carpenters whose houses I live in. All around me are the traces and memories of the dead. We live among the dead, until we join them.

How is faith to endure, O God, when you allow all this scraping and tearing on us? You have allowed rivers of blood to flow, mountains of suffering to pile up, sobs to become humanity's song—all without lifting a finger that we could see. You have allowed bonds of love beyond number to be painfully snapped. If you have not abandoned us, explain yourself.

We strain to hear. But instead of hearing an answer we catch sight of God himself scraped and torn. Through our tears we see the tears of God.

A new and more disturbing question now arises: Why do you permit yourself to suffer, O God? If the death of the devout costs you dear (Psalm 116:15), why do you permit it? Why do you not grasp joy?

FOR A LONG TIME I knew that God is not the impassive, unresponsive, unchanging being portrayed by the classical theologians. I knew of the pathos of God. I knew of God's response of delight and of his response of displeasure. But strangely, his suffering I never saw before.

God is not only the God of the sufferers but the God who suffers. The pain and fallenness of humanity have entered into his heart. Through the prism of my tears I have seen a suffering God.

It is said of God that no one can behold his face and live. I always thought this meant that no one could see his splendor and live. A friend said perhaps it meant that no one could see his sorrow and live. Or perhaps his sorrow is splendor.

And great mystery: to redeem our brokenness and lovelessness the God who suffers with us did not strike some mighty blow of power but sent his beloved son to suffer *like* us, through his suffering to redeem us from suffering and evil.

Instead of explaining our suffering God shares it.

But I never saw it. Though I confessed that the man of sorrows was God himself, I never saw the God of sorrows. Though I confessed that the man bleeding on the cross was the redeeming God, I never saw God himself on the cross, blood from sword and thorn and nail dripping healing into the world's wounds.

What does this mean for life, that God suffers? I'm only beginning to learn. When we think of God the Creator, then we naturally see the rich and powerful of the earth as his closest image. But when we hold steady before us the sight of God the Redeemer redeeming from sin and suffering by suffering, then perhaps we must look elsewhere for earth's closest icon. Where? Perhaps to the face of that woman with soup tin in hand and bloated child at side. Perhaps that is why Jesus said that inasmuch as we show love to such a one, we show love to him.

MADE IN THE image of God: That is how the biblical writers describe us. To be human is to be an icon of God. This glory is one we cannot lose. It can be increased or diminished, though; our imaging can be closer or farther, more glorious or less. Authentic life is to image God ever more closely by becoming like Jesus Christ, the express image of the Father.

In what respects do we mirror God? In our knowledge. In our love. In our justice. In our sociality. In our creativity. These are the answers the Christian tradition offers us.

One answer rarely finds its way onto the list: in our suffering. Perhaps the thought is too appalling. Do we also mirror God in suffering? Are we to mirror him ever more closely in suffering? Was it meant that we should be icons in suffering? Is it our glory to suffer?

STANDING ON A HILL in Galilee Jesus said to his disciples:

> Blessed are those who mourn,
> for they shall be comforted.

Blessings to those who mourn, cheers to those who weep, hail to those whose eyes are filled with tears, hats off to those who suffer, bottoms up to the grieving. How strange, how incredibly strange!

When you and I are left to our own devices, it's the smiling, successful ones of the world that we cheer. "Hail to the victors." The histories we write of the odyssey of humanity on earth are the stories of the exulting ones—the nations that won in battle, the businesses that defeated their competition, the explorers who found a pass to the Pacific, the scientists whose theories proved correct, the athletes who came in first, the politicians who won their campaigns. We turn away from the crying ones of the world. Our photographers tell us to smile.

"Blessed are those who mourn." What can it mean? One can understand why Jesus hails those who hunger and thirst for righteousness, why he hails the merciful, why he hails the pure in heart, why he hails the peacemakers, why he hails those who endure under persecution. These are qualities of character which belong to the life of the kingdom. But why does he hail the mourners of the world? Why cheer tears? It must be that mourning is also a quality of character that belongs to the life of his realm.

Who then are the mourners? The mourners are those who have caught a glimpse of God's new day, who ache with all their being for that day's coming, and who break out into tears when confronted with its absence. They are the ones who realize that in God's realm of peace there is no one blind and who ache whenever they see someone unseeing. They are the ones who realize that in God's realm there is no one hungry and who ache whenever they see someone starving. They are the ones who realize that in God's realm there is no one falsely accused and who ache whenever they see someone imprisoned unjustly. They are the ones who realize that in God's realm there is no one who fails to see God and who ache whenever they see someone unbelieving. They are the ones who realize that in God's realm there is no one who suffers oppression and who ache whenever they see someone beat down. They are the ones who realize that in God's realm there is no one without dignity and who ache whenever they see someone treated with indignity. They are the ones who realize that in God's realm of peace there is neither death nor tears and who ache whenever they see someone crying tears over death. The mourners are aching visionaries.

Such people Jesus blesses; he hails them, he praises them, he salutes them. And he gives them the promise that the new day for whose absence they ache will come. They will be comforted.

The Stoics of antiquity said: Be calm. Disengage yourself. Neither laugh nor weep. Jesus says: Be open to the wounds of the world. Mourn humanity's mourning, weep over humanity's weeping, be wounded by humanity's wounds, be in agony over humanity's agony. But do so in the good cheer that a day of peace is coming.

"IF THE GOD who revealed life to us, and whose only desire is to bring us to life, loved us so much that he wanted to experience with us the total absurdity of death, then—yes, then there must be hope; then there must be something more than death; then there must be a promise that is not fulfilled in our short existence in this world; then leaving behind the ones you love, the flowers and the trees, the mountains and the oceans, the beauty of art and music, and all the exuberant gifts of life cannot be just the destruction and cruel end of all things; then indeed we have to wait for the third day."

HENRI NOUWEN,
A Letter of Consolation

PERHAPS THERE'S something more in what Jesus meant. Not only is there a new day of peace coming. To those who mourn the absence of that day is disclosed already the heart of God. Upon entering the company of the suffering, they discern the anguish of God. By this anguish they are comforted. Upon joining the crowd on the bench of mourning, they hear the sobs and see the tears of God. By these they are consoled.

> Those who sow in tears
>   will reap with songs of joy.
> He who goes out weeping,
>   carrying seed to sow,
> will return with songs of joy,
>   carrying sheaves with him.
>   PSALM 126

WHAT IS SUFFERING? When something prized or loved is ripped away or never granted—work, someone loved, recognition of one's dignity, life without physical pain—that is suffering.

Or rather, that's when suffering happens. What it *is*, I do not know. For many days I had been reflecting on it. Then suddenly, as I watched the flicker of orange-pink evening light on almost still water, the thought overwhelmed me: I understanding nothing of it. Of pain, yes: cut fingers, broken bones. Of sorrow and suffering, nothing at all. Suffering is a mystery as deep as any in our existence. It is not of course a mystery whose reality some doubt. Suffering keeps its face hid from each while making itself known to all.

We are one in suffering. Some are wealthy, some bright; some athletic, some admired. But we all suffer. For we all prize and love; and in this present existence of ours, prizing and loving yield suffering. Love in our world is suffering love. Some do not suffer much, though, for they do not love much. Suffering is for the loving. If I hadn't loved him, there wouldn't be this agony.

This, said Jesus, is the command of the Holy One: "You shall love your neighbor as yourself." In commanding us to love, God invites us to suffer.

GOD IS LOVE. That is why he suffers. To love our suffering sinful world is to suffer. God so suffered for the world that he gave up his only Son to suffering. The one who does not see God's suffering does not see his love. God is suffering love.

So suffering is down at the center of things, deep down where the meaning is. Suffering is the meaning of our world. For Love is the meaning. And Love suffers. The tears of God are the meaning of history.

But mystery remains. Why isn't Love-*without*-suffering the meaning of things? Why is *suffering*-Love the meaning? Why does God endure his suffering? Why does he not at once relieve his agony by relieving ours?

WE'RE IN IT TOGETHER, God and we, together in the history of our world. The history of our world is the history of our suffering together. Every act of evil extracts a tear from God, every plunge into anguish extracts a sob from God. But also the history of our world is the history of our deliverance together. God's work to release himself from his suffering is his work to deliver the world from its agony; our struggle for joy and justice is our struggle to relieve God's sorrow.

When God's cup of suffering is full, our world's redemption is fulfilled. Until justice and peace embrace, God's dance of joy is delayed.

The bells for the feast of divine joy are the bells for the shalom of the world.

"Put your hand into my wounds," said the risen Jesus to Thomas, "and you will know who I am." The wounds of Christ are his identity. They tell us who he is. He did not lose them. They went down into the grave with him and they came up with him—visible, tangible, palpable. Rising did not remove them. He who broke the bonds of death kept his wounds.

To believe in Christ's rising from the grave is to accept it as a sign of our own rising from our graves. If for each of us it was our destiny to be obliterated, and for all of us together it was our destiny to fade away without a trace, then not Christ's rising but my dear son's early dying would be the logo of our fate.

Slowly I begin to see that there is something more as well. To believe in Christ's rising and death's dying is also to live with the power and the challenge to rise up now from all our dark graves of suffering love. If sympathy for the world's wounds is not enlarged by our anguish, if love for those around us is not expanded, if gratitude for what is good does not flame up, if insight is not deepened, if commitment to what is important is not strengthened, if aching for a new day is not intensified, if hope is weakened and faith diminished, if from the experience of death comes nothing good, then death has won. Then death, be proud.

So I shall struggle to live the reality of

Christ's rising and death's dying. In my living, my son's dying will not be the last word. But as I rise up, I bear the wounds of his death. My rising does not remove them. They mark me. If you want to know who I am, put your hand in.

"By his wounds we are healed." In the wounds of Christ is humanity's healing.

Do *our* wounds also heal? This gaping wound in my chest—does it heal? What before I did not see, I now see; what before I did not feel, I now feel. But this raw bleeding cavity which needs so much healing, does it heal while waiting for healing? We are the body of Christ on earth. Does that mean that some of our wounds are his wounds, and that some of our wounds heal?

Is our suffering ever redemptive? I suppose the blood of the martyrs sometimes was. It was an instrument of God's peace. But my suffering over my son, which I did not choose and would never choose: does that bring peace? How? To whom?

Is there something more to say than that death is the mortal enemy of peace? Can suffering over death—not living at peace with death but *suffering* in the face of death—bring peace?

"MORTIFICATION—literally, 'making death'—is what life is all about, a slow discovery of the mortality of all that is created so that we can appreciate its beauty without clinging to it as if it were a lasting possession. Our lives can indeed be seen as a process of becoming familiar with death, as a school in the art of dying. I do not mean this in a morbid way. On the contrary, when we see life constantly relativized by death, we can enjoy it for what it is: a free gift. The pictures, letters, and books of the past reveal life to us as a constant saying of farewell to beautiful places, good people, and wonderful experience. . . . All these times have passed by like friendly visitors, leaving [us] with dear memories but also with the sad recognition of the shortness of life. In every arrival there is a leavetaking; in each one's growing up there is a growing old; in every smile there is a tear; and in every success there is a loss. All living is dying and all celebration is mortification too."

—HENRI NOUWEN,
A Letter of Consolation

SUFFERING MAY DO us good—may be a blessing, something to be thankful for. This I have learned.

Ordinarily we think of the powerful and wealthy as blessed; they enjoy the "good things of life." But maybe the little ones, the downtrodden peoples and assaulted persons, are blessed as well. I do not mean that they will be compensated for their sufferings. I mean that perhaps the treading down is itself a blessing, or can become a blessing, rich as any coming to those we call "the lucky ones."

Suffering is the shout of "No" by one's whole existence to that over which one suffers—the shout of "No" by nerves and gut and gland and heart to pain, to death, to injustice, to depression, to hunger, to humiliation, to bondage, to abandonment. And sometimes, when the cry is intense, there emerges a radiance which elsewhere seldom appears: a glow of courage, of love, of insight, of selflessness, of faith. In that radiance we see best what humanity was meant to be.

That the radiance which emerges from acquaintance with grief is a blessing to others is familiar, though perplexing: How can we treasure the radiance while struggling against what brought it about? How can we thank God for suffering's yield while asking for its removal? But what I have learned is something stranger still: Suffering may be among the *sufferer's* blessings. I think of a former colleague who, upon recovering from a heart attack, remarked that he would not have missed it for the life of him.

In the valley of suffering, despair and bitterness are brewed. But there also character is made. The valley of suffering is the vale of soul-making.

But now things slip and slide around. How do I tell my blessings? For what do I give thanks and for what do I lament? Am I sometimes to sorrow over my delight and sometimes to delight over my sorrow? And how do I sustain my "No" to my son's early death while accepting with gratitude the opportunity offered of becoming what otherwise I could never be?

How do I receive my suffering as blessing while repulsing the obscene thought that God jiggled the mountain to make *me* better?

SUDDENLY HERE he is again. The chain of suggestion can begin almost anywhere: a phrase heard in a lecture, an unpainted board on a house, a lamp-pole, a stone. From such innocuous things my imagination winds its sure way to my wound. Everything is charged with the potential of a reminder. There's no forgetting.

HIS YOUNGER brothers had begun to ask him for advice. To Claire and me he had become an equal, no longer a child to be cared for. Now he's gone, and the family has to restructure itself. We don't just each have a gap inside us but together a gap among us. We have to live differently with each other. We have to live around the gap. Pull one out, and everything changes.

It's been a year now since I last saw this small patch of earth. Then it was piles of dirt and a hole. Now I can scarcely tell. Then it was surrounded by teared humanity. Now just mother and father, sister and brothers. The gardeners are gone, the neighborhood children are gone, only the wind in the oaks abides.

He was sealed—no, his *body* was sealed— in a zinc box. How do the worms get in? Or do we each provide our own worms, carried along inside us? How much have they gnawed away by now? The bones will last a long time, and I suppose the clothes. I had gone through his closet and picked out a shirt and pants in his favorite colors. I imagine some of it was artificial fiber, and that lasts longer, doesn't it? I suppose the buckle on his belt will last a long time, too. Shoes? No, they gave me his shoes. He doesn't have shoes on.

I walk around the patch where he was buried, not over it nor onto it. Why do I do that? Walking on it seems like desecration. I begin to understand why humanity has regarded its burial grounds as sacred sites. Under each of these plots has been laid to rest what remained of one of God's images on earth, one of his icons. Those icon-remains hallow this place.

I suppose if that's true, then the houses of the living are even more hallowed. If the resting places of the remains of God's icons deserve respect, then surely the dwelling places of his living icons do. The grass here is nicely mowed, the rolling hills lovely, splendid oaks, very peaceful. I suppose some of those buried here never lived so well.

I wonder how it will all go when God raises him and the rest of us from the dead? Giving us new bodies seems no great problem. But how is he going to fit us all together into his city? Eric here, man of the twentieth century, has to be fitted in with someone from long ago who lived in primitive conditions, knowing nothing of airplanes and electricity and neutron bombs, knowing only of the patch of soil which she tended and from which she never strayed more than five miles. Will God have everyone learn computers? Eric would have a head start. And what about the different characters and temperaments that all these people bring? Eric was loyal and gentle and loving, if sometimes a bit self-centered. Some people are nasty, ill-tempered, unpleasant to be around. How will God handle that? Seems to me there'll have to be a lot of purging first.

And so many, so innumerably many. I see them stretching way back, their faces eventually becoming just a brownish haze from here. Everybody is known by somebody in that crowd, but the memories usually trail off somewhere so that up front here we know only a very few. God alone has them all in mind.

I don't see how he's going to bring it off. But I suppose if he can create he can re-create.

I wonder if it's all true? I wonder if he's really going to do it?

Will I hear Eric say someday, *really* now I mean: "Hey Dad, I'm back"?

"But remember, I made all this, and raised my Son from the dead, so. . . ."

OK. So goodbye Eric, goodbye, goodbye, until we see.

"WE MUST BE STILL and still moving
Into another intensity
For a further union, a deeper communion
Through the dark cold and the empty deso-
lation,
The wave cry, the wind cry, the vast waters
Of the petrel and the porpoise. In my end is my
beginning."

T. S. ELIOT,
Four Quartets

Appendix

In honor of their son Eric, Claire and Nicholas Wolterstorff commissioned composer Cary Ratcliff to write a requiem, to a text which they composed mainly from biblical passages. The first performance of *Requiem: Eric Wolterstorff in Memoriam* was given on May 18, 1986, in Grand Rapids, Michigan.

Following is the text. Part I expresses the awfulness of death. Part II is a lament. Part III affirms that we are not alone in our suffering, but that God shares it with us. Part IV is what Eric himself might say. Part V expresses the endurance of faith. And Part VI speaks of Christian hope.

Requiem

Part I

Truly terrible is the mystery of death.
I lament at the sight of the beauty
created for us in the image of God
which lies now in the grave
without shape, without glory, without
    consideration.
What is this mystery that surrounds us?
Why are we delivered up to decay?
Why are we bound to death?

JOHN OF DAMASCUS

There is hope for a tree if it be cut down,
    that it will sprout again
    and its shoots not cease.
But we die and disappear.
    We breathe our last, and where are we?

JOB 14

Never again do we return home;
    our dwelling place knows us no more.

JOB 7

Part II

Like a bird alone in the desert
    or an owl in a ruined house
I lie awake and I groan,
    like a sparrow lost on a roof.
Ashes are the bread that I eat,
    I mingle tears with my drink.

PSALM 102

From the depths I cry to you, O Lord,
    give heed to my lament.

PSALM 130

Does the grave declare your great love?
Is your truth proclaimed in the tombs?
Are your wonders admired in the dark
    or your mercy where all is forgotten?

PSALM 88

Why do you turn away?
Why do you hide your face?
I wait for you, my soul waits,
    and in your word I hope.

PSALM 130

Restore me, O God my Savior.

PSALM 85

Part III

In all our afflictions he is afflicted,
    and the angel of his presence saves us;
in his love and pity he redeems us;
    he lifts us up and carries us all our days.

ISAIAH 63:9

He bears our griefs
    and carries our sorrows;
by his wounds we are healed.

ISAIAH 53:4, 5

Part IV

In my beginning is my end
In my end is my beginning

T. S. ELIOT

O Lord, you have fathomed and known me;
    you know when I sit down or stand;
    you created my inmost parts
    as you wove me within the womb.
You saw me before I was born,
    my days were inscribed in your book;
    they were all formed and set
    before a single one came to be!

PSALM 139

My heart is not proud,
my eyes are not haughty;
I am not intent on great things
nor achievements sublime.
My soul lies at rest
as quiet as a child;
my soul is as still as a babe
at its mother's breast.

PSALM 131

I depart in peace
for my eyes have seen your salvation.
You have shown me the path of life.
In your presence there is fulness of joy,
in your right hand are pleasures forevermore.

PSALM 16

In justice I go to behold your face;
I shall find joy in your likeness when I awake.

PSALM 17

Part V

Our days are like grass;
    we flourish like flowers of the field;
    the wind passes over and we are gone,
    and our place knows us no more.
But the steadfast love of the Lord abides
      forever.

PSALM 103

Though the fig trees do not blossom
    nor fruit be on the vine;
    the produce of the olive fail
    and the fields yield no food;
though the flock be cut off from the fold
    and there be no herd in the stalls,
yet will I rejoice in the Lord;
I will joy in the God of my salvation.

HABAKKUK 3

Part VI

We have seen a great mystery:
We shall all be changed.
We shall be raised in Christ
    as we were buried in Christ.
Death is swallowed up in victory.
The dwelling of God will be with his people.
God will wipe every tear from their eyes;
    and death shall be no more.
      There shall be no mourning, no crying nor
        pain;
      sorrow and sighing shall flee away.
For the old things are disappearing.

REVELATION 21

The poor will be raised from the dust;
    the sorrowing, lifted up from their ashes.

SONG OF HANNAH

Those who sowed in tears
shall reap with songs of joy.

PSALM 126

For the word of the Lord is peace.

PSALM 85

"Behold, I am making all things new.
I am the Alpha and the Omega,
the beginning and the end."

REVELATION 21